Beyond
the
Brink

Tiffany Chew Floyd

authorHOUSE®

AuthorHouse™
1663 Liberty Drive
Bloomington, IN 47403
www.authorhouse.com
Phone: 1-800-839-8640

Published by AuthorHouse 10/30/2014

ISBN: 978-1-4969-4996-7 (sc)
ISBN: 978-1-4969-4995-0 (e)

Library of Congress Control Number: 2014919223

All you can

Don't stop believing even when you have done all you can
Put your faith in God
He is not like man.
God can do anything
So lift your head to the sky.
Before one tear falls
Before you breathe one sigh
Know that with each prayer Jesus is nigh

Stand in the face of adversity
Arch your back to the wind
Hold your head up to the heavens
God gives you a hand and lends
You love in your heart
Take the step to start, your
Faith walk today
When you feel you've done all you can
Kneel and pray.

Allegiance

I pledge allegiance to my Jesus, the One who set me free.
I pray that I can be, Lord, your hands and feet.
Going into the world and shining the light
That comes in my life; because of my relationship with Christ
I want to tell a dying world
That there is hope
Jesus Christ is where I put my faith
Believing in my heavenly Father and knowing
How great, he has bestowed inalienable rights to me
Now I am compel,
To shout and yell
This world that sometimes can seem destitute and alone
It is time to sing a new song
Believe when you pray
Down in your heart
Our heavenly Father has been with us from the start
Now what must we do with our lives
But be God's lights
Shine your light for the entire world to see
Give God your best
He has made you free
When you tell of your faith
The world will learn. He is great.
By your testimony
Be the hands and feet
Tell everyone you meet
That we serve a Mighty God
Live your life as a light
Make the world bright!
Shine for all to see.
Live in your destiny.

Anchor me

I will not be moved.
This defeat will not be in me.
I made the mistake
My spirit does break
Pain and scars
Life's wounds
Hard lessons
Tears and strikes
Untold confessions
Free my spirit!
God, give me life
I can.
I will
Do what's right.
No longer just a hearer
Jesus draws me nearer.
Heaven I long to see
I will touch my destiny.
I will not be moved.

Blank Canvas

A clear script
A blank page
An open window
A transparent stage
An open door
An empty room
A budding flower
A fresh bloom
Flourish, blossom, and grow
The word of God I need to know.

Can't Do It Alone

Some have goals.
Some have dreams.
Few have vision.
Only one has the means.
People try to make it on their own.
But no man can do it alone.
God does have a plan for all.
Who will answer His call?
Not everyone believes.
Those are the ones that don't achieve.
Some people think they can do it alone.
They end up confused and never reach the throne.
Your goals and dreams,
You should trust the One who has means
He knows what it takes.
He knows all your reams.
He knows what's inside of you.
God formed you in your mother's womb.
God knows the plans he has for your life.
Turn it over to Him and walk in the light.

Color

Tisk the dawn of a new horizon
Searching for the midpoint
Streaks of gold, orangey meridian
Hoping for a real one
Values of hue cover the sky
Whimsical pleasantries capture my eye
Vivid ah shades, shades of hue
Meridian melody
Saying I do
Lights to dark
Fade like the shutting of an eye
Values of hue
Beauty in the sky

Decorate Your Soul

Decorate your soul.
Don't put your life on hold.
Prepare, plan, and get busy watch your life unfold.
Pray to the one true King and watch Jesus bring
You into a marvelous life,
It begins when you shine your light.
Decorate your soul!
Your story is waiting to be told.

Fading Away

The fading away of ashes from the stench of the debris
The faint torched smell that surrounded the sea
The fire in the water and the smoke on the sand…
That was the downfall of the sinful catamaran.
Drifting out in the ocean with no charted course
The sinful catamaran was destined for remorse.
The night loomed with peril. The catamaran rebelled.
Sailing amidst the tumultuous waves, it needed a lifeline
Only one can save.

Flower

How do I feel now, I need to know?
I want so bad to change,
But haven't planted a seed to grow
Change to a better flower
I need a rain shower.
Not a mist that sours
I need a cloudy, rainy day to wash my dirt away
And then a clam and dry breeze to replenish my leaves
I need fresh ground soil
So my roots don't spoil
For too many a time or two
I have dealt with dew
And in due time
I pray that my mind be renewed.
For like a flower my mind needs
A shower of the Lord's touch
To help me to grow
A presence of God
To touch my heart
A replenish to my soul
So I may be rooted in the word
I need direction, protection and the Lord's way of reflecting to me
The way I should be
For I have been wrong in the past
And I know it can not last
I need a seed to grow
Start over new
Lord, I pray and ask to hear a word from you.

"Hope in God's Promise"

In life we make decisions.
God gives us provisions.
We learn and pray.
We concentrate, on God's unchanging word.
We watch and we pray for this world today.
It has so much disarray.
People everywhere are going astray.
There is so much chaos and dismay.
We wonder when, Lord; You're coming back again?
And until that hour, until that time
Lord, I pray keep my mind.
Keep my heart
Fixed on You
Jesus without Your hope
Nothing matters and no one can cope.
The weary ways of this world…
We pray and believe
That hope we received
One day sweet, Jesus
You'll come back and retrieve, all who believe.

In His Hands

Sometimes you wonder why?
What could you have done differently?
Instead of worrying and wondering start praying and pondering;
What it is God wants from you in this moment?
Love God with your whole heart.
He'll put you where you need to start
In the right direction
God gives reflection and protection
Like only the Father can
Lay your head back and rest.
Put an end to stress.
Know that it's in God's hands.

Journey

Life is a journey
Walk with Jesus for safe travel.
You will never walk alone.
Keep your light aglow.
Let it shine and grow.
With Jesus on your side
Your life will be just fine
Life's journey alone
There would be no song
So hold onto God's unchanging hand
God can heal our land.

Let There Be

In time I see what can and will be
Lord shine your light on my destiny
I pray lead me on
Make me strong
Lead me not in temptations
Correct my wrongs
Give me a heart
Jesus, a heart like yours
So my love transcends; And it floods
I want to tell the world of all you've
Done for me
Given me boldness
And courage
Through adversity
You, Jesus have shined your light
On my life
You brightened it up
Illuminated my nights
How a love that showed
Way back on Calvary
Can still unlock the mental chains
And set souls free
How does one tell the world what you did for me?
I put pen to paper
And let there be

Let Your Light Shine

Let your light shine.
No matter what the weather
Is outside; you can have joy in your heart.
The Light of the world came to save
And to anyone who believes in Him, He gave
You a light
Let your light shine for the entire world to see
Sometimes the world can be a dim place
That lacks enlightening qualities
So choose today and forever more
To lighten, brighten and implore
Your light for the entire world to see

Liberty

In my mind I find the hope which floats.
I sense it in my dreams and sometimes breathe it in my soul.
I know that God is in control and he has a plan for my life.
To be destined to write, the story and combine
When I envision it in my mind
The blueprint, outline that I long to be fruition.
This is my quest, my expedition.
I will touch my destiny.
In God, I walk in liberty.

Life Is Like an Ocean

Life is like an ocean.
The waves come to shore,
Sometimes with a roar
But God's unchanging hand
Can lift you up again

Life can be like an ocean,
Hard times are like the waves crashing.
You pray and attempt to wade through the waves
But sometimes the water crashes and caves.
Never stop praying.
Keep trusting and saying, God will bring you out.
Just like a surfer on a surfboard,
God can guide you to life's reward.

The surf's not always up
And life's not always a beach.
Never get so high up that your knees don't reach the floor.
God will always bring you safely to shore.

Life's Lesson

In life you learn lessons.
Never forget your blessings.
People will come in your life
And people will leave.
Don't wear your heart on your sleeve.
This journey called life you will experience change
Some people won't stay
So your direction may rearrange
In life you have to learn yourself
Knowing God is your greatest help
You learn what helps you grow
You must stay focus and know
There's a time to reap
There's a time to sow.
God is with you every step of the way
Learn His voice and always pray
People will sometimes give unwanted advice
But only you can live this life
You only get one
Sometimes you regroup
Sometimes you feel stomped
In life you should learn lessons
Sometimes you have regrets
Sometimes you have confessions
On this journey called life
You won't always get it right
But get understanding
Life can be demanding
In all you do live
Live, love, and give
You learn on the journey
Don't stress unnecessarily
You don't get out alive
So stress sparingly

Life's Journey

The journey of life has twists and turns.
No one can prepare you for the bend in the road.
You try and listen if you're told
But the journey is to be all your own
What lies ahead for some; is not the same
For you, we all are on a journey in life,
We all hear a different tune.
Life's journey can be an adventurous place
I began my journey
Every morning with a cup of grace
I pray at night. God be my light.
I pray in the day
Lord, lead the way.
Sometimes I have forgotten to pray
Those days of life's journey were not okay.
I thank God for this journey of life.
I let go of all strife.
I pray that your journey on the road ahead
Is filled with God's blessings and your soul is fed.
On my journey, I seek Godly wisdom and inner peace.
I pray my journey ends with sweet relief.
To one day call heaven my home.
On life's journey
We are never alone.

Love waits for you

Love shines its light through
Love makes a bridge to your heart
Love is there at ever part
Love is the story you share
Love brings joy and laughter
and it bares any heartache or sorrow
Love can wait and sometimes walks away
But true love
No one can ever take

Renew

Life is what you make of it.
You get what you put into it.
When one plays games, the game plays for keeps.
Instead renew your mind because; the word still speaks.
You have a path; you have to choose.
Choose the game and you always lose.
Choose the word, it's a two edged sword, use it wisely and it goes forth.
The word is a sword that's mightier than a weapon.
When God's on your side; you can keep on stepping!
Step up!
Walk in a different direction.
Map out a plan that strives for perfection.
Live in a new standard of life.
Choose what you need. Make the sacrifice.
For this life however temporal, you still have to live.
It's not measured in what you get.
It's measured in what you give.

Running

Running on empty
Walking on stilts
Maneuvering through the murky world,
I don't want to end up in the pits.
Trouble comes in all shapes and forms

Running on empty
Walking unfulfilled
I must keep going
I can't stay still

Running on empty
Reeking from the weight
Revving in my imagination
I've got to anticipate,
Something better to come
I'll find that stretch of highway
Where my heart runs free
I see, a better me

Walking slow
Running steady
Times speeding up
I am not ready
Leaving it behind
Leaving as quick as I can
I put my trust in God.
I fear no man.

In A New Season

God has given me another chance.
Everyday I live I must advance
And enhance to a higher call.
Lord, I give you my all.
I'm in a new season.
I have a reason
And a right to praise Him,
The one, true God
Our living Savior
On my life
He's given me favor.
I thank God in advance.
I'm in a new season.
I have a million reasons
To give thanks
Even if I don't fill in the blanks
Looking over my life
God has kept me through
Good times and through strife.
I'm in a new season.
I believe and decree!
I know our God
Is blessing me.

Seeing Beyond the Brink

Looking to the sky, I feel the wind on my skin.
Disappointed by the way of the world
Lord give me a fresh wind.
Start over new.
Replenish my faith today
Please forgive me for my sin.
Please hear me when I pray.

Looking toward the sky
Standing tall and strong
Trying to arch my back
Yet, I know I've done much wrong
Hide me behind the cross
Shame my face in dcw

Looking to the sky I find time to brcathe
To inhale a sense of freedom
I wonder and believe
To face my failure head on
To know that I have tried
I look toward the sky and
Know one day I will fly

Tarry

Things began and things end
Time goes on and we make amends
The year goes by and the days vary.
We have little time
So we must carry
A heavy load
"The race is not given to the swift nor the strong."
So we must pray and tarry long.

The Brink

You can change; when you rearrange the way you think.
You take the time to renew your mind
You can do anything!
Jesus says, "Come as you are."
All you have to do is start.
Take the first step.
And you won't regret.
Jesus is the best.
He is a present help.
He gives you another chance.
When you trust in him
You can have a life full to the brim.
See beyond the brink.
Jesus loves you always
Even more than you think.

The Cross

Sitting in the moonlight
I stare into the night sky
I feel the breeze on my hand
I know God's grace has taken me in
I see the glare and glow of the moon
Jesus I know you will return again someday soon
I sense your presence around me
Open my eyes so I may see
This world I know it can be a desolate place
But Jesus your love and saving grace
Tells me to prepare
My faith is great
Oh how I long to see your face
I pray that all who has an ear to hear
From close by and far
All draw and gather near
For the time at hand
We shouldn't fear
But in our hearts be of good cheer
For those who are believers in Christ
He promises us everlasting life
And though some days are as dark as night
Jesus is our shining Light
So let the light shine in you
Take up your cross in all you do
Let the world see Him in you

Think Before You Act

In sequence
In hue
In focus
In view
Plain sight
Double vision
Wrong move
Indecision
Quick thought
Long time
Ponder right
Made mind

Ties that Bind

Eight years ago a song was written
Lyrics were relevant
And two races represented,
Two races collaborated
To make something
That united the soul
Young minds and young hearts
Grabbed the Grammy world's attention
And took hold,

The song was about a natural disaster
That the magazines and media plastered
All over the tv and internet
Blacks and whites
Got upset
Races have had ups and downs
Although at the core
We're all human
Yet we tend to store
Animosity in certain situations
So much hurt
So much degradation
Fast forward
Eight years later
Things are now enraged
Races disengaged
Tragedy is man made
Our history so torn
It roots from slaves' days
Yet in some minds
Some will never be free.
God did create us, human
He created you.
He created me.
We no matter what race

Are here in one place
When will we seek God's face?
And not His Hand.
Learn to fear God
And no man
Only God has a heaven or hell to put you in
Racism is just one of many sins
It's time to wake up and get your mind right
I pray that no matter what color
You learn to walk in light.

Tiffany Chew Floyd

Time

Time waits for no one.
Days fly like the speed of light.
When you are a certain age,
You should want to do what's right.
People tend to do what feels good
But that isn't always best.
At the end of the day it can leave
You restless…It has come a time that
Mankind needs to examine his and her self.
Know what is right and live to help.
Not everyone will make it to heaven
But it should be your goal. We are appointed to die
Who will save your soul?

With You

I live and believe.
The air that I breathe
The scenery that I see
Everything that is within me
I know God is there.
He surrounds us in the atmosphere.
He created our being
Speaking in an existence of more than one
The spirit of the living Son
I embark on a new quest
My journey is a test
Lord, help me to be my best
Live and breathe through me
I'm a vessel; an instrument renew me now
Lord, Jesus show me how
To love again
With You on my side
In life I win.
A life brand new
Only am I, complete with You.

Word

Root me in the word, not just what I heard.
Reading to acknowledge God's ways
We are living in the last days
Learn the word.
Read and believe.
God's grace I do receive.
I will not be moved.
Be still. Be quiet, wait
Praise God each and every day.
Don't be moved from your place.
Seek God's face.